REROUTED FOR GREATNESS

How Life's Detours are Setups for Your Greatest Success

Aisha Ritchie

Printed in the United States of America.

ISBN: 978-1-966723-49-3 (paperback)

Acknowledgement

I must first express heartfelt gratitude and praise to God for His faithfulness over the course of my life. He has and continues to be a lamp to my feet and a light to my path.

To my book coach, Crystal Daye, and the DayeLight Publishers team, thank you for your support and for believing I could do this, even when I doubted it myself. You have helped me to turn a simple thought into something that will leave a legacy for generations to come. Your prayerful and practical support, guidance, and direction will forever be appreciated.

To my son, Malik, who sat with me night after night while I wrote, constantly reminding me of God's faithfulness. As you read this book one day, may you know how blessed you are and continue to be a blessing to those around you.

To Leroy James, who planted the idea of writing a book about my journey six years ago. Your support means everything to me.

Finally, to Dr. Tasheney Francis, my sister and confidant, thank you for your constant love and prayerful support.

As you read, may you also be reminded that God is our ever-present help along our rerouted paths and He always redirects us to something greater.

Table of Contents

Acknowledgement iii
Introduction 7
Chapter 1: When Life Throws You A Curve Ball 11
Chapter 2: Navigating The Unknown 23
Chapter 3: Recalculating Route: From Panic to Possibility. 33
Chapter 4: Surrendering to the New Path 43
Chapter 5: Finding Your True North 61
Chapter 6: Navigating Fear and Self-Sabotage 71
Chapter 7: Building Resilience and Antifragility 93
Chapter 8: Step Into Your Greatness 103
Conclusion 117
About the Author 121
References 123

Introduction

This is probably not the life you planned.

You may have envisioned how everything should have turned out: the job, family, lifestyle. Everything may have been clearly set out in your thoughts and even your plans. You knew where you were going and even prepared for your desired path until you experienced a collision with your destined path, and it's not the one you planned.

Maybe it was a loss you never saw coming, a decision that did not turn out as you hoped, a delay that lasted way longer than you expected, or a door that closed without explanation. The journey you trusted may have suddenly disintegrated, leaving you to navigate unfamiliar and unwanted territory.

If this sounds like you, then this book is for you.

This book was written for those who have felt like their lives have been completely derailed. It feels like you have faced hardship after hardship, adversity after adversity, and see no clear path to restoration. You may even have given up and embraced a defeated life, quietly thinking that your detours disqualify you from greatness and success. This book will remind you that it has not.

Detours do not mean that you are behind, that you have failed, or that you have been forgotten. Detours mean that something new is being formed within you—something powerful, formidable, and great.

Throughout this book, we will have honest conversations about the discomfort of being rerouted—the fear, the battles, and the temptation to give up—but you will also see how this discomfort is purposeful, character-building, and serves as a training ground for something greater. You will encounter personal stories from my own journey that highlight the detours, redirections, and all the messy pieces in between.

This book will help you reframe your setbacks as divine detours meant to set you up for your greatest success. It will reframe obstacles as hidden strategies that prepare you for greatness by offering mindset resets and perspective shifts. Most importantly, this book is about deciding to move.

While reflection matters and awareness is powerful, action is transformative. Each chapter is designed to

help you not only understand but also appreciate your journey whilst engaging with it, so you do not remain stuck or trapped in your rerouted season.

Life has been preparing, stretching, and strengthening you for what comes next. The detour was never your final destination; it was just your training ground.

By the time you get to the end of this book, my hope is that you won't just see your journey differently, but you will see your future with greater expectancy.

Let's begin the journey.

Chapter 1

When Life Throws You A Curve Ball

Award-winning theatre producer, Actor Boy Awards and Phoenix Awards best lead actress nominee, major television commercial contracts, regional voice-over projects, my first feature in an award-winning international film, job promotions, and so much more—2018 and 2019 were shaping up to be the best years of my life.

It was amazing. I felt amazing. I was winning. Until, BOOM! A positive sign on a pregnancy test changed everything.

What?! This had to be wrong!

So, I tested again, and again, and again, but nothing changed.

I was pregnant!

How could I let this happen to me? What would I tell my parents? What would I tell my church? How would I explain this to the Youth Fellowship and Praise Team that I was leading? My whole world crumbled in that moment. The success trajectory I was on felt like it had all crashed and burned.

I remember that day like it was yesterday. I sat in that bedroom with a whirlwind of emotions rushing through my mind and body. I was shocked, embarrassed, disappointed, and confused. I felt lost, I was literally trembling, and all I could do was bawl (a very extreme and intense cry in Jamaican Creole).

I remember taking up the cell phone and calling my prayer and accountability partner, whom I call my big sister. In a frenzy, unable to articulate myself clearly, I cried, attempting to explain to her with the little words that came from my mouth that I was pregnant.

"I can't do this. I won't do this."

Then it hit me! I knew the answer: I would get rid of it.

"Tash, I'm going to get rid of it."

I had decided. It was final. I would never let this dark little secret see the light of day. I would terminate, and nobody would know that it ever happened. Nobody!
I recall her encouraging me and praying for me, expressing her support with whatever decision I would ultimately make. Her response was shocking. It was not what I expected to hear. I guess I was expecting her reprimand, but somehow her calm compassion and composure lessened my turmoil. After my conversation with her, I was a little less frantic but still in shock and panic.

Still a little dazed, I called my pastor. Believe it or not, it was easier for me to call my pastor than my mother because I had no idea how to face her. Although I was a 30-year-old accomplished young woman, this felt like a teenage pregnancy, and in my Jamaican household, a teenage pregnancy was no joke. I was never to become a statistic. Yet, here I was feeling like one.

I told my pastor I needed to talk to him about something urgent. He heard the tears, panic, and urgency in my voice and immediately scheduled a meeting, which would take place a few days after the call.

That night, as I tried to go to bed, I was restless. It felt like the weight of the world was on my mind. I couldn't sleep, so instead I lay in bed, eyes red, with tears running down my face. The cries had to be silent because I was living with my mother and could not afford for her to ask what was wrong with me.

Unable to sleep with silent tears running down my face, all I could think about was what I needed to do to keep this little secret forever. I remained resolute that I would abort the child, and nobody would know anything. Then I heard a voice, as clear as day, "*And then what?*"

I was confused. Did I accidentally say something out loud that my mom might have heard? I knew I didn't, so who or what could hear my inner thoughts? *Could it really be... Nah!* I quickly shut down the thought, convincing myself of my unworthiness. There was no way this could be the Holy Spirit.

I heard it again, *"Abort and then what?"* I was now conflicted, and tears started to flow even more, as the sobbing intensified.

Feeling unworthy of God's presence, I tried to run away from it, to ignore it, thinking it would probably go away. I just wanted to stay numb. Then I heard for a third time, "*Abort and then what?*"

I got up, went to the bathroom (my primary prayer room), and cried before the Lord. How could He still be trying to talk with me after what had happened? I responded, *"Nobody will know."*

He said, *"I will know."*

Guilt and shame rushed through my body, and in frustration and anger, I asked, *"So what am I supposed to do?"*

He said, *"When you abort, you will make the enemy win."*

I responded, *"He's already won."*

He corrected me in His love and said, *"What if I can use this? I will create something beautiful out of your mess."*

I felt like this was one of those cliché things you always hear Christians say: *"God will turn your mess into a message."* So, was it actually God, or was I just hearing what I thought I needed to hear in that moment?

I was still confused and overwhelmed, so I hesitantly and angrily prayed for clarity, asking the Lord to tell me if this was really Him. I remember daring Him to change my heart and mind about the abortion, if it really was Him, and help me to navigate the situation if He could really turn this mess into a message.

I continued crying, went back to my room, closed the door, and pondered everything bad that might happen until sleep came in the wee hours of the morning.

The next morning, I woke with one thing on my mind: *"I will create something beautiful out of your mess."*

On my lips, I woke involuntarily singing the lyrics of the chorus, *"Something beautiful, something good, all my confusion He understood. All I had to offer Him was brokenness and strife, but He made something beautiful out of my life."*

I kept repeating this chorus over and over again, as the tears started rolling down my cheeks once again. I knew what it meant. I knew what I had to do. I didn't understand what *"something beautiful"* meant or what it would look like, but those thoughts lingered in my mind all day, so I accepted it and leaned into God's reassuring promise.

I decided to keep the baby.

Sharing with my pastor and church leaders was hard. Sharing with my family was harder. I felt like I was not going to make it. I felt like my life was literally about to end. But as I look back six years, I am so happy that I embraced this redirected path.

Sometimes life takes us in the complete opposite direction of our plans. We want to achieve what we want. We want to chase our dreams. We want to live our best lives, sometimes based on societal pressures. With social media so prevalent now, it has gotten even worse. I know it is hard, but I want you to pause for a moment and contemplate this: C*ould these redirections be paths to discovering your true purpose? Could these be stepping stones to set you up for something greater? For something beautiful? Could these off-course moments be divine detours orchestrated by God to lead you into His desired path for your lives? Could these detours lead you to your true destiny?*

This year, I took the time to map out my personal journey, and I have recognized that my life has not gone the way I planned, yet it has gone exactly as it should.

Throughout this book, I will share parts of my journey with you and the lessons I have learned as I trod my rerouted paths. I will share how life's detours are set-ups for your greatest success and how leaning in and embracing them can be the greatest blessing of your life.

John 13:7 explains, *"You do not realize now what I am doing, but later you will understand." (NIV)*. Jeremiah 29:11 tells us *"For I know the plans I have for you," declares the LORD, "plans to prosper you and not to harm you, plans to give you hope and a future." (NIV).*

Put simply, God knows what He is doing. He created each of us with something bigger than we can even think or imagine inside of us.

Sometimes, in our own haste to achieve success and fulfill our desires and dreams, which don't necessarily align with God's plan for us, we go off course, thinking it's the right way, but God's purpose will prevail. Just think about Jonah, who got swallowed by a whale and still had to carry out God's mission (see Jonah 1–2).

This is why we experience these redirections and divine detours. This is why He allows us to stumble sometimes, so that we can look to Him. This is why He reroutes our paths to lead us into our great destinies, which He already prescribed for us (see Ephesians 2:10).

You may feel like everything in life is going completely wrong. You may have experienced setback after setback, and you can't seem to see the light at the end of the tunnel that everyone is talking about. You've experienced hardships, missed big opportunities, dropped out of school, studied and worked hard, but didn't get the promotion, done a million interviews, but still can't seem to land the job. You have tried so many things that just seem to always fail, so you've just given up.

You put on a brave face every day, but deep down, you struggle with self-doubt, regret, and the haunting fear that life has passed you by. You probably also wonder if the setbacks in your life mean that you were just born to suffer.

No! You were born for greatness. Greatness is embedded in the fibre of your very being. Don't give up! Don't settle!

Everything you have experienced in life has brought you to this point for a reason. It has shaped who you are for a reason. Your unique value—that thing that makes you stand out and makes you special—is staring you in the face.

It's time to unlock the purpose of your rerouted path.

As Rick Warren says in his book *A Purpose-Driven Life,* the only person who can tell us what is the purpose of our life is the one who gave us life, so ask Him.

Your setbacks are not dead ends; they are divine detours leading you to the path God has set for you. Trust the process.

He's got you!

Key Takeaways

1. Greatness is embedded in the fibre of your very being.
2. Your unique value—that thing that makes you stand out and make you special—is staring you in the face.
3. Your setbacks are not dead ends; they are divine detours leading you to the path that God has set for you.

Rich Reasonings

Take a look at your journey.

Identify important milestones in your life (the good, the bad, and the indifferent) and map out your journey to where you are currently. Remember that every experience in our lives has shaped us into who we are today. This exercise will help you gain clarity on where you are coming from, so you can connect the dots to where you are now and where you want to go.

MY JOURNEY TO GREATNESS

A Step-by-Step Review of My Path

Chapter 2

Navigating The Unknown

As humans, we crave stability, certainty, and ease. We want answers, timelines, and guarantees. We also want life to have a clear path that is characterized by a straight line from dream to reality, with predictable steps along the way. This is why so many rely so heavily on GPS systems every day. We want to avoid traffic, roadblocks, and other interruptions along the journey to our destination to ensure the best, smoothest possible journey.

Unfortunately, life does not travel in straight, smooth paths all the time. Instead, in most instances, it feels like a recalculating GPS that constantly reroutes us through unfamiliar territory, unexpected delays, and roads we sometimes don't know and/or never planned to travel. This is where the discomfort begins—the unknown. It is the unsettling place that strips us of control and forces us to admit that we do not have all the answers.

Unknown territory puts us in a space where our plans may no longer be valid, and our confidence feels a little shaky. Neuroscientists share that when we do not know our next move, our brains often react as if we are in danger, our body releases stress hormones, and this heightens anxiety and fear within us. Put simply, when we are uncertain, we don't just feel uncomfortable; we feel unsafe. Yet, some of the most defining moments of our lives are born in these very spaces. Deciding to keep the baby and navigate the pregnancy journey was one of those moments for me.

On paper, I was qualified to handle life. I was a mature young woman with an MBA, a solid career trajectory, and a reputation built on excellence, faith, and leadership. But none of that prepared me for the emotional weight of navigating an unplanned pregnancy as an unwed Christian woman in a highly visible faith community.

The Christian community knew me. I was the church girl who served in several ministries within my local church and other national bodies. I was the singer in a gospel band that once shone in the gospel music industry. I was the girl who mentored several young

people who had an interest in pursuing Christ. My Christianity was loud, and now, with no ring on my finger, my pregnancy was about to take the spotlight.

I was not just dealing with physical changes; I was navigating whispers, internal shame, and the fear of judgment. How people knew me and how I knew myself were being challenged all at the same time.

I had told my pastor that I wanted to personally advise my local church community before anything showed or before any rumors surfaced. He wanted to support me with the announcement, but this was something I had to do for myself and by myself. The situation was not about to change my transparency, so he obliged.

Standing in front of my church that Sunday afternoon on August 4, 2019, was one of the most terrifying moments of my life. I was trembling on the inside, but concealed it with a brave face for all to see. No one was expecting what I was about to say.

I had played the scenarios in my mind countless times in the days preceding my announcement: what I would say and how I would say it. I even imagined potential responses that would follow, yet being scared cannot even begin to describe how I felt on that day.

I stood and shared, *"...I am pregnant!"* There... I told them. The room went still. The silence that followed my announcement was not empty; it was loud and heavy. I could feel the weight of shock, confusion, disappointment, and compassion all sitting in the same room.

As I took my seat, an entourage of young adults stood in my defense. An older church sister approached me, embraced me firmly, and warmly encouraged and prayed with me.

With an entourage of friends and young adults surrounding me, I sat as my pastor made closing remarks. To be honest, I have no idea what he said, as I was lost in my own thoughts and feelings. This moment marked the beginning of my journey through the unknown season of pregnancy and motherhood, one I was not prepared for.

I knew the months ahead would be uncomfortable. I knew there would be stares, quiet conversations, and even moments where I would question myself. I felt like I was about to go through a very lonely period, regardless of the support I had from my partner, family, friends, and well-wishers, but it was my journey, and I had to walk it no matter how I felt.

While emotional and attempting to process everything, the one thing I could think of was the One who told me that He would use this situation for my good. I still had no idea what good could come from it, but I trusted Him. So, I did the only thing I could: I went back to God.

Acknowledging that I could not do it on my own or in my own strength, I prayed that He help me to navigate what was about to be a very new, uncertain, and uncomfortable journey. I admitted that even if no one said a word, my own thoughts were loud enough to overwhelm me. I did not ask for everything to make sense. I simply prayed for His peace. In fact, that's all I can remember praying for: that His peace abounded. Repeating Philippians 4:6-7 and John 14:27, I simply craved His peace, so that I could be steadied to walk this new path with His guidance. That prayer changed everything.

I was held by His peace, and as a bonus, He added grace, mercy, and continuous demonstrations of His unconditional love. This combination brought me through nine months of complete ease. My pregnancy was smooth: no complications, illness, issues, cravings, aversions, not even pain.

His peace and grace allowed me to worship weekly at the same local church I had served in all my life for the entire nine months of my pregnancy, with almost no condemnation, and where there was, He shielded me from it.

His peace allowed me to continue stage theatre and work throughout the nine months without fear or concern about my health. His peace allowed me to sleep comfortably at night, knowing that He was my guide.

The same journey I thought would break me was quietly strengthening me and preparing me for something greater, something I did not yet see or believe could happen in my future. I would never have imagined that out of this circumstance, I would be thrust into purpose as an author, speaker, and coach. I would never have thought that the situation would be the impetus that pulled me out of mediocrity and revealed a life of abundance through my renewed faith in God.

It taught me that the unknown is not meant to be navigated alone. We were not designed to carry life's uncertainty in isolation. We were designed for communion with God and meaningful community. So, be intentional about what you do and who you are surrounded by in your unknown and uncertain seasons. Find people who will help you navigate well, destiny

helpers who will walk with you and steer you in the direction that God is leading you. People who will pray with and for you and help you to see God's best when you can't even see it for yourself.

We desire a full map with detailed, clear steps before we even commence the journey, but life often reveals direction one step at a time. This means the unknown is inevitable and forces us to slow down, listen, and trust someone beyond our limited understanding.

Looking back, I recognize that this detour, while a consequence of my actions, was preparation for my next season. It built my resilience, whilst developing my reliance on God. God did exactly what He promised: He created something beautiful out of my mess. It was not just the birth of a wonderful baby boy, but the birth of a stronger, more connected woman.

There are moments in life when being off-course is exactly what we need. This is not meant to confuse or harm us, but to build and reveal our true strength while forcing us to acknowledge its source. These unknown spaces are often the very spaces where purpose becomes clear.

If you are currently navigating the unknown and feel uncertain about the path ahead of you, be assured that you are not abandoned. It might not feel like it, but rest assured, you are being led. Even in the deepest valley and darkest of nights, help is present because He promises never to leave or forsake you (see Deuteronomy 31:6).

You don't have to have all the answers. You don't have to figure it out all on your own. All you have to do is walk by faith and seek His peace, the peace which surpasses all understanding. Believe that the One who grants you this peace is always there.

The unknown can be scary and feel unsafe, but it is not a dead end. It is a doorway to your greatest success.

Key Takeaways

1. The most defining moments of our lives are born in these very [unknown] spaces.
2. The unknown is not meant to be navigated alone; we were not designed to carry life's uncertainty in isolation.
3. There are moments in life when being off course is exactly what we need. This is not meant to confuse or harm us, but to build and reveal our true strength.
4. The unknown is not a dead end. It is a doorway to your greatest success.

Rich Reasonings

What "unknown" season are you trying to navigate right now?

____

____

____

____

____

Where have you been trying to control outcomes instead of trusting the process?

____

____

____

____

What might this detour be preparing you for?

____

____

____

____

____

Chapter 3

Recalculating Route: From Panic to Possibility

The Cambridge Advanced Learner's Dictionary and Thesaurus describes panic as *"a sudden strong feeling of anxiety or fear that prevents reasonable thought and action."* It causes us to think irrationally, cripples action, and usually leads us to hold on to the fear of uncertainty.

During periods when we feel our worlds have been turned upside down, most of us experience panic. I know I did when I saw repeated positive signs on those three pregnancy tests. A flood of emotions overtook me: anger, disappointment, terror. All I could think of was doom and gloom. So, in my moment of irrational thinking, my brain told me to do the next best thing to get over those feelings: abort the baby.

See, that's the thing: panic causes such an intense, sudden, and overwhelming fear that it impacts our usual behaviours and thought processes. In my case, the action I thought of was a quick fix. In some cases, panic might leave us feeling overwhelmed and doing nothing about it.

How many times have we experienced a rerouted path that just stops our lives—we are alive, but we aren't really living. We simply exist.

Does any of this sound familiar?

- You dropped out of school because you had to become the family's primary breadwinner.

- You lost a family member unexpectedly, which completely flipped your world.

- You got fired from the job that you dedicated so much time working in and building.

- You work consistently hard in the job, hoping to be awarded that upcoming promotion, only to have an outsider who you are expected to train land the job.

- You're in a serious relationship for several years, expecting marriage, but the relationship ends in shambles.

- You married the person you thought was the man/woman of your dreams, but the marriage ended almost as soon as it started.

I could go on and on… What do you do? With all the pain and panic that you experience in all these and other situations, what do you choose to do?

Sometimes, we sit and sob about life and all the bad things happening to us. We sometimes become so comfortable with our discomfort that we live in a bed of pity and invite friends over to join the party. We stop living. We stop caring. We give up.

I want to challenge that thought and those actions (or the lack thereof). Instead of seeing your circumstances as closed doors, why not see it as God's redirected path: a pathway to purpose.

I'm not at all saying we shouldn't address the emotions we experience in these uncomfortable situations. Trust me, I know it is critical to address these, as they form the foundation for building back stronger. But I also want us to think about the possibilities that can come from our pain and panic.

I once heard someone say that pain from failure offers an opportunity to see and experience better outcomes—it offers an opportunity to thrive.

Nona Jones, in her book "The Gift of Rejection," shares that greatness and mediocrity are separated by one thing: how you respond to rejection.

It is extremely hard to find positives in moments of rejection and disappointment. In fact, scientific research suggests that rejection and disappointment evoke a range of negative emotions. Scientist Mary Beckman, in a 2023 article, posits that "*the brain responds to social rejection in the same way it responds to physical pain.*"

So that 'sticks and stones' thing we learned as kids is a big fat lie: words hurt, rejection hurts, disappointments cause us pain, and if we are not careful about how we view them, they will also lurk and cause us to live unfulfilled lives.

The pains and setbacks I have experienced have taught me that, to succeed in life, I have to yield to and accept the imperfections of my life. Our success is rooted in the lessons we have learned from our failed (life-altering) experiences. When we embrace what we perceive as failure, it offers an opportunity to expand ourselves. We gain invaluable insights into what happened and learn how to move forward, stronger and better than before. It's not rejection; it's recalibration.

Maya Shankar, a cognitive scientist and TED Talk speaker, once shared that "*When an unexpected change happens to us, it can also inspire a lasting change within us,*" highlighting the transformative power of change.

I experienced this transformation firsthand in high school, on the path to becoming Dr. Aisha Ritchie. I was married to the idea of becoming a medical doctor for a while because it sounded good. It was part of the esteemed career group, and it would be great for bragging rights. I could just picture my now-late grandmother sharing with her friends and some family members, too, *"My granddaughter is a doctor."* Never mind that I hated blood, have an extremely low pain tolerance for myself and others, and squeal every time I am to get an injection or see one given. None of that mattered because it sounded good and I'm sure it would look good on my family and me.

I always excelled at school, and it was time to transition from lower school to upper school, which meant selecting the subjects for the CXC CSEC exams (the academic exams taken at the secondary/pre-tertiary level in the Caribbean region). There was no other path; it was clearly the Sciences, so naturally I applied and got in for all except Biology (Really, Mrs. Ellis?!). But it was fine, I spoke to my dad about it, and we agreed that I would just do it privately. No roadblocks for me: I was on track to become Dr. Aisha Ritchie.

So, you can imagine my frustration and dismay when I returned to school that September, only to be told that my file had somehow been mixed up and that all my classes were now linked to Business Studies. *What?! How could I be the only student with this mix-up? Doesn't a mix-up suggest that at least two students (myself and someone else) had challenges? So how was I the only one?* None of it made sense to me.

Annoyed and frustrated, I spent hours trying to get into the Science groups, but they were all full. I remember my Vice Principal saying to me, *"Aisha, just go and sit in the business classes. Who knows, you might choose to stay."*

Stay?! Really, Ms. Morrison?!

I did not want to stay. I wanted to become Dr. Aisha Ritchie (not the PhD type). My grandma was supposed to brag about me being a medical doctor. *Was I the only one getting this? Hello?!*

Annoyed, frustrated, and disappointed, I sat in my first business class: Principles of Accounts. It felt as if my dreams were fading away. I remember the teacher

asking us to introduce ourselves and state why we chose to study Accounts. When I was asked, I gave her so much attitude (thinking about it now, it was rude) and told her and the rest of the class that this was a temporary inconvenience. I told them I did not choose to be there, making it clear I had no interest in being there. It was a mix-up that would soon be resolved. I was 'in my feelings,' and in that moment, I didn't care about how anyone else felt. This was a roadblock that needed to be cleared.

After four weeks of business classes with no positive updates from the school administration, it was clear that this was my new path. I was forced to pivot, and I even found that I wasn't bad at it; in fact, I was really good at it. From very early on, I was one of the students who did extremely well at grasping the concepts, even helping other students understand these subject areas better. So, it was no surprise that I excelled in the CSEC and later CAPE exams, and received numerous awards for business studies, including top performer awards throughout my years of study in high school, was a part of the Honors Society while pursuing my undergraduate degree in Economics, and graduated with distinction at the master's degree level.

I even recall one year receiving five scholarship opportunities during my undergraduate years. God was good. My parents did not have to worry about paying for school; a way was already made. I guess I didn't think about the tuition part of things when I was on my Dr. Aisha Ritchie journey.

Fast forward twenty years, and I can share successes and failures in business, as well as my expertise in international business, business strategy, business development, and business risk management. I am now a chartered insurer and proud business coach and consultant who works with small business owners across the world to boost business income, increase profitability, and achieve sustainable success.

By embracing the shift from the Sciences to Business (after much resistance), I expanded my capacity and was redirected to my purpose pathway. It recalibrated my route and led me to God's desired destination. It provided the perfect detour for me to step into my greatness.

Unexpected or even unpleasant changes do not have to be an unwelcome redirection; if embraced, you will see that it is a setup for your greatest success. It's not a setback; it's a setup for greatness.

1. When we embrace what we perceive as failure, it offers an opportunity to expand ourselves.
2. Our success is rooted in the lessons we have learned from our failed (life altering) experiences.
3. Unexpected or even unpleasant changes do not have to be unwelcome redirections.

Rich Reasonings

Where are you currently experiencing pain or panic?

____

____

____

____

How can you separate your identity from this outcome and focus on who you are becoming? Think about the qualities that you are developing through this challenge.

____

____

____

____

How can you honour your emotions while still choosing to move forward with hope? Give yourself space to feel what you feel, then write a letter, prayer, or personal mantra that will help you to rise to the day.

Chapter 4

Surrendering to the New Path

Believe it or not, your life is happening in the exact way it should.

I've come to appreciate and understand that nothing that happens in our lives is arbitrary, nothing—the missed alarm, the traffic delay, the missed opportunity—absolutely nothing!

So many of us question whether things are happening at the pace they should or even in the way they should, but be assured that everything is happening how and when it should. As Jamaicans put it, '*Nuttin nuh happen before de time*' (nothing happens before it's time) and '*What is for yuh cyaa be unfi yuh*' (what is meant for you cannot be given to anyone else).

I wasn't always like this. In fact, if you are anything like the way I used to be, you would have visualized, planned, and mentally organized how everything in your life is supposed to happen.

At age eighteen, I sat down one day and planned my life. I decided that by age twenty-five, I was supposed to be married with two children, living in a mansion with 'name brand' cars (preferably Mercedes-Benz) parked in the garage, while my family and I overlooked the city of Kingston, Jamaica. I'd take my parents out of the ghetto and set them up in a beautifully furnished contemporary home with everything they desired. I'd travel all over the world speaking to large audiences and vacation travel to my heart's content, with no worries about finances, and would have a foundation set up in my name to give back to vulnerable youth in Jamaica. Like Martin Luther King Jnr., I had a dream!

So, you can imagine my dismay when I turned twenty-five and was still living with my parents, trying to find a sound footing in a corporate job, working for a company that kept promising promotions with nothing forthcoming. This was not supposed to be my life!

Over time, I've learnt that life does not conform to our rigid plans and timelines. How can it? We are not the masters of time; God is, and I have come to appreciate that everything He does is done with intention.

Romans 8:28 reminds us that *"...all things God works for the good of those who love him, who have been called according to his purpose." (NIV)*. We can trust that no matter how difficult, challenging, or even weird the path may seem, we can embrace it knowing that the One who controls the universe has made a way for us.

Proverbs 3:5-6 implore us to *"Trust in the Lord with all your heart and lean not on your own understanding; in all your ways submit to him, and he will make your paths straight." (NIV)*. It simply encourages placing complete faith and reliance in the all-knowing God, rather than relying on our own understanding or short-sighted knowledge.

I once heard my pastor, Rev. Claude Ellis, say, "*We can trust in the unfailing and unchanging hand of God because He is conscious, capable, concerned, and consistent.*" This speaks to God's character. Sometimes He will take us on a journey we don't understand, but because we can trust His character, we know that the detours or reroutes are meant to build something within us that aligns with our greatness and success.

In Psalm 23, it says that though we walk through the "*Valley of the shadow of death,*" He is with us. I'll never forget the moment I really understood this scripture. A shadow can only be formed in the presence of darkness and light, so even when you feel like you are alone or you are derailed, there is light, and the presence of God remains with you always. The shadow is simply a cast. Science supports this by showing that a light source is required for a shadow to form.

See, the thing is, we are so short-sighted, but God has the best view of our lives; not only does He have a bird's eye view, but He is navigating and putting all the other pieces together to ensure that we fulfill what He has prepared us in advance to do (see Ephesians 2:10)—the fulfillment of our purpose. When you think about it, it really makes sense because, before we were even conceived, He knew us and set us apart for His unique divine purpose (see Jeremiah 1:5).

One of the things we must learn to do is release control. I know how difficult this is—believe me. We tend to want to control everything because we think we know what is best for us. We make plans, write goal lists, create vision boards, and go head-on about ticking these things off, sometimes without consulting God to see if that's what He wants for us. We want to hold the steering wheel and wish for a straight, smooth sailing path when we begin the journey, but sometimes the road is bumpy, sometimes there are twists and turns, sometimes there are roadblocks, sometimes there are detours that must be taken for us to get to the divine destination we are meant to reach.

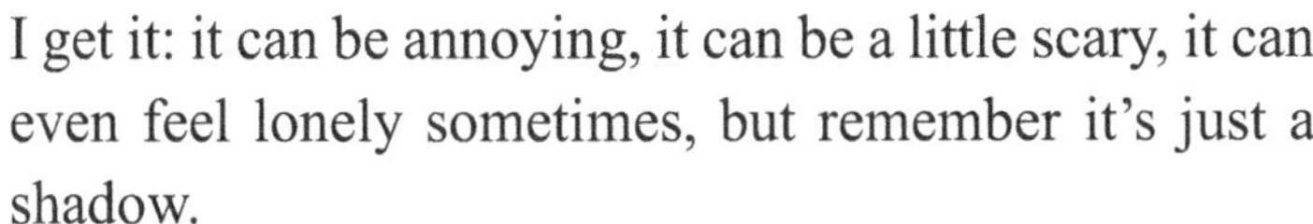

I get it: it can be annoying, it can be a little scary, it can even feel lonely sometimes, but remember it's just a shadow.

Graduating from the University of the West Indies with my undergraduate degree in Economics was a big achievement. I was the first in my immediate family to graduate from university, and I did so with honors. I graduated in the middle of the global financial crisis of 2010, when so many people were losing their jobs and there were hiring freezes everywhere. Nobody was hiring except call centers, and I was not about to spend all this time excelling in school to sit in a call center making minimum wage (at least, that's what I heard at the time). No disrespect meant to anyone working in a call center who is reading this book, but this is just really how I felt.

I applied for jobs like crazy, and I was fortunate to land quite a few interviews with recruiters in corporate, most of whom encouraged me to pursue my master's degree because I was "very bright." I thought about it for a while, but I could only get a partial scholarship for the MBA, and I couldn't afford the tuition at the time. Outside of that, I really didn't get it: *if I was "very bright," shouldn't you hire me then? How would I gain experience if you won't give me a chance to get it?*

Anyway, I remember being called by one of my high school business teachers. Yes, we stayed in touch and even became friends after I left high school. She told me there was a temporary contract available for an upper school teacher in the Business department. I quickly applied, and without hesitation, I was back at my alma mater, St. Hugh's High School, after three years of university; only this time I was a teacher of Economics for 6th formers, and Principles of Accounts and Principles of Business for 4th and 5th form students, and guess what? I loved it!

And before you even start to think it, no, it was not nepotism. While I was the top business student at the school and the head girl of the institution before I left, I now had a paper (the degree) that further proved my expertise—the job was mine.

Teaching lit me up. Outside of preparing lesson plans and developing classroom curricula, I loved it. It allowed me the opportunity to impact lives meaningfully, not just based on a syllabus; it was more than that for me. It provided me with an avenue to shape these students' lives holistically. My lessons were not just academic; they were life lessons. It brought me right back to when I used to teach "rocks and pebbles" as a child, and it felt fulfilling. Perhaps it shouldn't have been Dr. Ritchie after all.

So, you can understand that as the contract period approached its end, I was saddened. With no open vacancies within the Business unit, I had to start job hunting again. It was fine, though, because God favoured me. I believed that. He opened this door. I was confident that He wouldn't leave me hanging now, and oh, how He proved me right; within weeks of applying to different organizations, while teaching, I got a job offer from an insurance brokerage firm.

Did I know anything about insurance? Nope! Was that going to stop me? Absolutely not! All I needed to do was get in that room and demonstrate that I would be an asset to the company. So, that is exactly what I did, and they hired me.

I recall speaking to the Founder, Board Chairman, and CEO of the company, who called me personally. I remember him asking me to start within three weeks; that was in the middle of my syllabus conclusion for my CXC CSEC and CAPE students. I was not prepared to abandon them at this crucial period, so I declined the offer, advising that I could not start until three months later. Guess what? He waited. He waited three months for me to join his company. Wow, what a blessing. God had done it again!

So there I was, three months later. Stepping into that corporate office felt different but welcoming. I was open to learning about the world of general insurance, which I knew nothing about at the time, but I was a quick and curious learner, so I didn't foresee any challenges.

I started off as a simple Customer Service Representative, handling walk-in customers, phone queries, and processing simple auto insurance matters.

I recall the CEO asking me to complete a task that was usually handled by people at a junior to mid-management level or above. I did it, and he was pleased. So, he asked my then supervisor to assign me duties typically handled by junior and middle management personnel, while I carried them out alongside my regular work tasks; that was within my first month there. That felt good. I must have been doing something right, right?

The responsibilities grew steadily, and I outperformed one after another until I began giving presentations at the company's weekly management meetings. I missed teaching, but things were going well in the corporate space, or so I thought.

One day, the CEO asked me to modify a report, which I did, and I kept the modified version for future presentations. I remember this day like it was

yesterday: the CEO, senior managers, supervisors, and me (the little CSR) were all in a meeting. I presented, as I usually would, but this time something was different; I could feel it, but I didn't quite know what it was.

I recall the CEO questioning me excessively, and then the questions became exclamations. He told me I was "cooking the numbers." I reminded him, in my very bold, expressive 23-year-old tone, that he had asked me to make modifications and that we had been using the format presented since the previous week. I then experienced what I had heard others talk about: his bitterness. I'll never forget asking my immediate supervisor and the other managers in the room if they recalled his comments from the previous meeting, and everyone said "no." I had gone through my first 'corporate jungle' experience, and from that day on, he never treated me the same, and I was no longer invited to these weekly meetings.

Searching for jobs while I worked there was hard; it was as if God had forgotten that it was me, the one He favours. I felt stuck in an uncomfortable position and hated my job, though I still gave my best simply because of my character and core values.

One Friday afternoon at about 3:00 p.m., I recall the human resource manager coming to my desk and handing me a letter. I didn't open it because it had to be my confirmation letter, but it wasn't. When I opened it at about 4:00 pm, the only thing I saw was the word **termination**. I was completely taken aback; they fired me with immediate effect. The company waited three months for me, promoted me to a higher level of responsibility in three weeks, and then fired me three months later. HR couldn't explain; even the general manager (the founder's daughter) said I did nothing wrong and gave some story that pointed right back to that day in the meeting.

I walked out of that office at 5:00 p.m. on a rainy Friday evening on October 25, 2011. I walked to my taxi stand without an umbrella, and waited for a cab to get home, while rain splashed my face and tears ran down my cheeks, indistinguishable from the rain. I felt hopeless, despair, anger, and disappointment. Why would God have me go through all of that and then disappear? Why would He cause this ditch? Why?!

As I got home that day and reflected on everything that had happened, I quarreled with God. I was fine teaching; it was fulfilling. By now, I would have also learned that all my students, even the difficult ones, experienced success in their external exams. Why didn't He just open a door there? Why would He send me to be challenged at this insurance brokerage firm,

only to have me feel embarrassed at the end of the day? Why was He so quiet? I was confused and angry.
As I continued to apply day after day, month after month, I waited and waited; no callbacks, no interviews, nothing was forthcoming. I felt like a bum and a failurc.

The family's shining star and university honors graduate, who was supposed to be Dr. Aisha Ritchie, was fired and was now at home doing nothing. I questioned myself so many times. Did I peak early? This is something I had heard about. Was this now a downward spiral? Was I an imposter? Was anything going to change in my favour?

I can recall someone recommending to my mom that I should try to get a job in a wholesale Downtown. A wholesale? Really? Was I that defeated?

I waited another three-plus months (clearly the number three is a standout in my life), and those three months felt like three years. I finally got a call from a church that wanted to interview me for an administrator and project officer position. A church? It was one of the largest parish churches in the Kingston metropolitan area. I didn't even remember applying for such a job, but it was a call, so I went and got the job. I quickly accepted because I needed the money and the boost of confidence, however small.

While my time there was brief, I gained a lot of experience in some areas of business and project management that I had not foreseen at all. Another door opened, and it made more financial sense to go.

I was hesitantly heading back into insurance, but this time to one of the most well-known insurance companies in Jamaica with a regional footprint. I was timid. I did not have much luck the last time I worked in insurance, so what if the same thing happened here? But I went, and over a decade later, I still work in the general insurance industry. Two general insurance job changes later, I continue to serve and contribute to Jamaica's general insurance industry, and I have built a strong brand and positive reputation for myself in the industry.

Let me tell you something, God has a way of elevating you when you least expect it. The Bible says that the *humble shall be exalted and the boastful shall be humbled* (see Matthew 23:12). Remember that job that fired me? Would you imagine that three and a half years later, I was in a position at the insurance company I worked with at the time that required them to seek my approval to conduct some of the insurance businesses they needed to conduct? Just, wow. God is something else!

I remember having to visit there after my appointment to manage their portfolio, and I visited with my then-manager. I remember the look on the CEO's and general manager's faces when they saw that I was now responsible for their portfolio of businesses. As I was introduced, I recall the GM saying, *"We know that Aisha is an excellent resource..."* I smiled, not with pompous pride, but with awe at how God works. It was a full 360-degree moment for me. God took me there, three-plus years ago, allowed me to get fired three-plus months in the job, and brought me back in a more esteemed role three-plus years later.

I want you to understand and appreciate that your reroutes are not meant to harm you. God is intentional about all that He does. In moments of adversity, it can be hard to see what He is doing, but we can trust His unchanging hand and His character. We can trust that He is conscious, capable, concerned, and consistent.

Romans 8:28 reminds us that "*we know [with great confidence] that God [who is deeply concerned about us] causes all things to work together [as a plan] for good for those who love God, to those who are called according to His plan and purpose.*" *(AMP).*

This rerouted path has taught me to trust the process. The job loss broke me. I experienced massive hits to my self-esteem and confidence level, and even went through chronically crippling self-doubt. But as I overcome daily, I have come to understand and appreciate how God works.

The detours are divine; they are closed doors that protect us from self- and other-harm, lessons we would never have learned otherwise, and character-building moments that prepare us for what is to come. They are meant to take us to our greatest success, but it requires us to trust Him.

Today, I am still working in the insurance industry as a Chartered Insurer within the Chartered Insurance Institute in the UK and underwriting manager at the only publicly traded insurance brokerage firm in Jamaica. I have received numerous awards throughout my career: multiple performance and employee-of-the-year nominations and awards, and, more recently, a manager-of-the-year award, which has been a full-circle moment.

My insurance journey hasn't just been about learning and excelling in general insurance; it has also served as a powerful catalyst for character-building and personal and professional growth. It has exposed me to areas of business strategy, business development, operations management, people development, people management, project management, communications,

and so much more. Through this experience, I have gained both technical knowledge and emotional intelligence, along with other essential soft skills, assets I carry over into my own entrepreneurial ventures.

Now, as a manager in my 9–5 job, an international speaker, a business coach, an author, and a creative, I have been able to weave all my experiences, knowledge, and God-given gifts together to motivate and mobilize individuals to step into their own greatness. My mission in life is to help others see the tremendous potential they have, no matter where they started off in life. Look at me, I was simply a little girl from the ghetto who has been able to climb the ranks and accomplish many successes.

Isaiah 55:8–9 reminds us, *"For my thoughts are not your thoughts, neither are your ways my ways," declares the LORD. "As the heavens are higher than the earth, so are my ways higher than your ways and my thoughts than your thoughts." (NIV).*

Your plans are minuscule compared to what He has planned for you. You are able to trust Him because He loves and cares for you. He holds the blueprint to your life; your role is simply to surrender to His plan. It's not failure, it's forging work—pressure that shapes your purpose into power.

"For I am about to do something new. See, I have already begun! Do you not see it? I will make a pathway through the wilderness. I will create rivers in the dry wasteland." Isaiah 43:19 (NLT)

Key Takeaways

1. Sometimes detours must be taken for us to reach the divine destination we are meant to reach.
2. Your plans are minuscule compared to what He has planned for you. You can trust Him because He loves and cares for you.
3. It's not failure, it's forging work—pressure that shapes your purpose into power.

Rich Reasonings

Could there be a "new thing" resulting from a rerouting that God is trying to use to unlock your greatness?

Chapter 5

Finding Your True North

We live in a culture obsessed with linear progression. From childhood, we are conditioned to believe that success follows a predictable trajectory. We grow up hearing this idea (though sometimes spoken silently) that life is supposed to follow a straight line: go to school, get a job, find love, live happily ever after. After all, that's what we read in books and see in Hallmark films. The problem with this narrative is that it ignores one fundamental reality of life: life is messy. Life does not move in straight lines; it twists, turns, doubles back, and sometimes forces detours that feel utterly directionless.

I was about ten years old when my father said, *"Ritchie, only three ways can take you out of the ghetto: talent (the Arts), sports, or a good education."* My ticket was education, and I never looked back.

At twenty-nine years old, I was a master's degree graduate. I had completed an MBA with a specialization in international business from one of the best business schools in the English-Speaking Caribbean, The Mona School of Business and Management, and graduated with distinction. I raised the bar yet again for my family and community.

I was proud of myself for this amazing accomplishment, but something was still missing. I couldn't understand it, and I felt a little ungrateful for all the sacrifices my family made for me to get to this point, but I couldn't shake the feeling of unfulfillment, so I hid it. After all, so many people would have wanted to be in my position. I was 'outside', I was 'doing the most': producing and acting in award-nominated and award-winning stageplays and films, serving as a youth ambassador, leading regional and national financial boards for the church, now in a progressive 9 – 5 job where my contributions were recognized and rewarded: I was doing great…or so it seemed to everyone looking in from the outside.

The thing is, I was doing what everyone thought was the right thing for me, everything that society said that I should pursue based on my talents and skill sets, everything that would make my family and friends happy and proud. Don't get me wrong, as a

multipotentialite, I enjoyed and loved doing these things. I was passionate about them, but it didn't feel like enough.

I was the strong friend everyone needed me to be, but I felt lost inside. I felt stuck, and I didn't even know what to do about it. After all, if I showed them my vulnerabilities, would I still be that strong friend? The promising daughter? The community star? Or would it all fade away? I was afraid of appearing not to have it all together. I was afraid of being ungrateful.

But there were other things that I wanted to achieve; things outside of my trajectory at the time. I wanted to write books. I wanted to speak on international platforms. I wanted to empower others to never settle and keep pushing to become the best version of themselves. I wanted to be the female Les Brown and Alvin Day, international leaders and speakers I liked and looked up to from my teenage years. It was no longer Dr. Aisha Ritchie; it was now international speaker and best-selling author, Aisha Ritchie. That was my new dream.

But I didn't think that path existed for me based on everything I was doing at the time, and, truthfully, I doubted my ability to achieve them because I didn't think I was good enough. Little did I know that what I was experiencing was something called *imposter syndrome.*

For a very long time, I had put myself on the back burner and played small. I was putting other people and their needs before my own, and I was fearful of stepping into the spaces I had dreamt of occupying. But in 2021, for the first time in about ten years and since being fired from that insurance brokerage firm, I stood face-to-face with my biggest setback: ME!

Stephanie Booth (Health and Wellness Specialist) and Smitha Bhandari (Medical Doctor) explain in a published article that imposter syndrome occurs when we doubt our own skills and successes. We feel we are not as talented or worthy as others believe, and we are scared that one day, people will realize that.

My imposter syndrome was rooted in fear: fear of failure, fear of criticism, fear of the unknown, and fear of success. Yes! I was even afraid to succeed because I pondered the changes that would come, and that was scary too.

I had become relatively comfortable with the 'ordinary' life I was living. So why would I uproot something that was going well? As I said, I made slow and steady progress in my career and was highly

regarded in my family and community. After all, it is said that slow and steady wins the race, right? Wrong! When you are not living out your full God-given potential and purpose, the sense of fulfilment will always evade you.

After learning about imposter syndrome and identifying some of the traits in myself, I knew that I needed to break the cycle. I needed to choose me. Yes, I made the decision: I chose me at thirty-three! Choose me? Except, I had no idea what that looked like or what that meant. I was so stuck in the idea that I was fine and so fearful of making uncomfortable moves that I didn't even know what choosing me meant. My vision was blurred, and I needed to change my lens. This required me to seek God for direction. So, I did, and He steered me back to my true north and opened an avenue for me to pursue a redirected path: my first book, *Choosing Me: 33 Inspirational Quotes*. Without recognition, I was fulfilling a teenage dream of writing a book of quotes, something my mom reminded me I wanted to do after I published. Something I had committed to God a long time ago and forgot about.

I also spent time building and expanding a community of people who could lift me up and hold me to a higher standard—people who helped me own my purpose and take responsibility whilst holding me accountable. I invested in coaching, which elevated my mindset and my personal brand.

New lens enabled me to see with a sharper vision and a fresh perspective. It pushed me out of my comfort zone and challenged me to live authentically, meaningfully, and purposefully.

In 2022, when I published my first book, simply out of obedience to God, I had no idea it would open the door to a professional international speaking career. I had no idea I would conduct workshops and speak to global audiences that would transform people's lives. I had no idea it would open doors to facilitating corporate training and to influencing meaningful change. I had no idea that such a tiny little book would reach the hands of so many people across the world, who have shared several testimonials about the positive impact that those words have had on their lives and their children's lives. All of this, simply because I chose to give birth to what the Lord had already called me to and equipped me for. Simply because I chose to embrace this unknown redirected path.

The bravest thing we can do is question the narrative we have been told and dare to write our own story. There is something powerful about realizing that life does not owe us a straight path because the truth is, we

were never promised one. John 16:33 informed us that *"In the world you have tribulation and trials and distress and frustration; but be of good cheer [take courage; be confident, certain, undaunted]! For I have overcome the world. [I have deprived it of power to harm you and have conquered it for you.]" (AMPC).* While Deuteronomy 31:8 reminds and encourages us, *"Do not be afraid or discouraged, for the Lord will personally go ahead of you. He will be with you; he will neither fail you nor abandon you." (NLT).*

Once you accept that, you begin to see the beauty in the messiness. Life isn't a straight line; it's a journey of detours, delays, and divine redirections. These detours, delays, and moments of doubt are not setbacks. They are setups for something greater because it is in those unexpected turns that God often places the very purpose we have been searching for all along.

My journey taught me that fulfillment does not come from checking off society's boxes or even from achieving great things; it comes from aligning my life with my true calling. This begins when you stop playing small, stop silencing your dreams, and start choosing to live with courage, clarity, and conviction, even when it scares you.

If you are feeling stuck, confused, or feel like you are falling behind someone else's timeline, let me remind you that you are not lost; you are being led. Maybe it is not where you thought you were going, but exactly where you need to be. Don't give up on your dreams just because they don't fit the world's ideal. Don't silence your calling because it looks different from everyone else's. Your purpose is yours alone.

Lean into discomfort. Speak life into those dreams that you have kept hidden for too long because now is the time to choose you, not out of ego, but out of obedience to the voice inside you that won't be quiet. That voice? It's your true self trying to break through.

Listen to it, then walk boldly into who you were made to be.

"*Live by design, not by default.*"
—Aaron Sansoni

Key Takeaways

1. When you are not living out your God-given potential and purpose, fulfillment will always evade you.

2. These detours, delays, and moments of doubt are not setbacks; they are set up for something greater because it is in those unexpected turns that God often places the very purpose we've been searching for all along.

Rich Reasonings

What are you passionate about? What lights you up?

____

____

____

____

____

____

Name three things that make you feel fulfilled and why.

____

____

____

____

____

____

What do others repeatedly seek your guidance or advice about?

____

____

____

If today were your last day on earth, what would you most regret not doing?

____

____

____

____

____

____

____

Has the rerouted path created something within you that you can now apply to your life in a meaningful way?

____

____

____

____

____

Chapter 6

Navigating Fear and Self-Sabotage

Choosing to accept God's purpose for your life and walking in it feels liberating. You finally know why you are here. You finally feel like it all makes sense (well, most of it). You finally get to pursue what lights you up. Finally! Until the doubts creep in.

You have stepped into your truth, declared your worth, and committed to the path that lights you up, but then, silence, hesitation, and the nagging voice that whispers: *"What do you think you're doing? What if you're not enough? Why do you think you're qualified to do this? Nobody will take you seriously. Nobody will listen to you. You're too broken to do this. What if you ruin everything by trying?"*

The truth is, choosing to live with purpose is only the beginning; the real work starts when you confront the invisible forces trying to pull you down and drag you backward: the fears, the lies from the enemy, the limiting beliefs, the habits that masquerade as self-protection but are really just self-sabotage in disguise.

It really doesn't matter how many vision boards you have made or how many affirmations you recite; if you want to truly move forward on this rerouted purpose path, you must identify and overcome the silent killers that may be holding you back from achieving your greatest success. After all, that's the point; remember, you are made to succeed.

After identifying my imposter syndrome, I participated in a group coaching programme that elevated my mindset and forced me to confront self-sabotaging habits I had developed over the years. I discovered that procrastination, negative self-talk, and comparison syndrome were my silent 'frenemies,' and they held on to me without much thought or recognition. I knew they needed to be booted.

Procrastination and Perfectionism

Procrastination is a silent killer. It is the act of delaying or putting off tasks until the last minute or past their deadline. It is not just a time management problem. Researchers suggest that it is *"a failure in self-regulation that leads us to act irrationally. We put*

things off, even though we know this delay will lead to negative consequences." (Kendra Cherry, 2025).

We tell ourselves, *"I can't start on a weekend." "Let me just start afresh next week." "I need to do some more work on this to make sure everything is perfect." "I just need a little more time to get this right."* The thoughts and excuses are endless.

The truth is, procrastination is less about timing and more about fear: fear of failure, fear of success, fear of proving the worst version of yourself right or what you think could be the best version of yourself wrong.

When we delay action, it is seldom because we do not know what to do or when to do it; it is usually because something inside us is whispering, *"What if I fail? What if I'm not ready? What if they don't like it?"*

I suffered chronically with this. If I'm being honest, sometimes I still do. I used to overthink and overplan everything. If I wanted to pursue something, my mind would tell me everything I needed to do or get before starting. I would have to research (Google and Chat GPT's advice were very important), then create a checklist or some 'working document' before anything actually started. My brain would go through this checklist before telling me it was okay to start or take action. If everything was not checked off, my brain told me to halt; I could not move forward because it was not yet perfect for me to begin. What a frustrating process! Just thinking about it now gives me a headache. This overcomplicated thought process literally slowed my path to excellence and even caused me to miss out on winning opportunities. Why? Simply because I was a perfectionist.

Perfectionism tells us the insidious lie that everything has to be flawless before we can start something or before it will ever be accepted by others. This causes us to wait forever on the perfect day, the perfect plan, and/or the perfect conditions to act, not realising that perfectionism is just another word for paralysis. It is very sneaky. It disguises itself as ambition, but it's really fear in a power suit.

I spent years writing business plans for what I hoped would be a model business consultancy firm within the Caribbean—writing and rewriting pitches, proposals, and strategy documents that never saw the light of day because they weren't perfect enough.

Perfectionism is not about excellence; it is about control, and ultimately, while we control some of the movements, God controls everything. The longer we try to remain in control and steer the wheel all by ourselves, the longer we take to experience true

success because we can make plans, but it is the Lord who establishes them (see Proverbs 16:9). Psalm 127:1 reiterates, "*Unless the Lord builds... the work of the builders is wasted.*" *(NLT).*

Life does not reward perfection; it rewards progress. Every masterpiece starts as a messy draft. Every breakthrough begins with a flawed attempt. Give yourself permission to be imperfect. Give yourself permission to grow.

True excellence allows room for growth, mistakes, and learning. Perfectionism demands flawless execution, not because the task requires it, but because our inner critic insists on it. It is not about doing our best; it's about controlling how we are perceived. It's time to heal from these thoughts, and healing begins when we trade control for courage and allow God to do the rest.

Perfectionism, which often results in procrastination, is simply a protective mechanism and survival tactic, but one that often keeps us stuck. Our brain would rather have us stay safely stagnant than risk the discomfort of growth. The good news is, once we name the fear, we can face it with faith, strategy, and grace.

How many dreams have you buried under the excuse of *"not being ready?"* I delayed writing my first book and even this one for a very long time because I convinced myself I needed more credentials, more experience, more time, more audience, but the truth is, I was terrified of being judged. So, I procrastinated.

Procrastination tends to thrive in fear. It is easier to live with regret than to face the possibility of failure, but I have learnt that action beats anxiety every single time. I once heard one of my mentors say, *"The antidote for fear is initiative."* The moment you start, those lingering doubts begin to lift, and the more you do, the more they fade.

In Economics, there's a principle called "opportunity cost." In simple terms, it is the value of a missed opportunity resulting from choosing an alternative. This can be financial or non-financial, but requires sacrificing one opportunity or action for another.

Ask yourself these questions:

What am I really waiting for?

____

____

____

____

____

____

What is the opportunity cost of waiting? What am I choosing to give up by waiting?

____

____

____

____

____

____

____

Negative Self-Talk

Have you ever heard a voice inside that said, *"You do not belong"* or *"You cannot do this?"* That annoying little self-critic is our relentless negative self-talk. Psychologist Elizabeth Scott, in a 2023 article, posited that negative self-talk is any inner dialogue we have with ourselves that may be limiting our ability to believe in ourselves and our own abilities, and to reach our potential. It is any thought that diminishes our ability to make positive changes in our lives or our confidence in ourselves to do so.

This voice often sounds like people who shared their doubts about themselves or us (directly or indirectly), especially in our formative years. This could look like teachers who dismissed your ideas, peers who told you that you were *"too much,"* or even well-meaning loved ones who told you to "be realistic" without recognizing that they had put down your hopes and dreams. Subconsciously, you may have internalised these statements, and now you may be thinking, *"I'm not qualified," "This is going to be too much for me," "I'm definitely not ready or cut out for this."*

Elizabeth Scott also shares that these negative thoughts may manifest in several ways:

- Grounded ("I'm not good at this, so I should avoid attempting it for my own personal safety.")
- Mean ("I can never do anything right!")
- Hopeless ("I don't deserve this.")
- Apathetic ("I'll fail anyways, so what's the point of trying?")
- Defeated ("That looks hard. Even if I tried, I'd never be able to do it.")

When these lies fester, they bleed into our choices, leading us to avoid opportunities that feel too big, too risky, too unfamiliar, or too uncertain. Instead of trying something new or challenging ourselves to grow, we say yes to safety and no to possibility, convincing

ourselves that playing small is the same as staying grounded.

Growing up in my teenage and young adult life, I was a very pretty, slender, bright, bow-legged young woman who didn't have to try very hard to walk like a model. That's right; I was beauty and brains (not to toot my own horn too much), but as I grew older, I became very self-conscious and even critical of my body.

I had a neighbour who constantly nagged and called me "mawga" (meagre). In the Jamaican context, this is far from a compliment; it often meant that someone looked very thin or even malnourished. This neighbour would see me every day, and, like a broken record, I would be teased about how "mawga" I was. This silently and secretly bruised my self-confidence. I started to believe what he was saying.

In my early 20s, I considered participating in both the Miss Jamaica World and the Miss Kingston and St. Andrew Festival Queen Competitions on multiple occasions, but my annoying self-critic kept reminding me that I was too "mawga" and not pretty enough to enter. I thought nobody would look at a "mawga" girl from the ghetto. Without intention, I had subconsciously accepted and started to believe the words the neighbour constantly spoke over me, internalized them, and now they were my reality—those borrowed thoughts became my own.

I was mean to myself; apathetic and defeatist thoughts consumed my mind: *"Don't even think about it. You'd never even make it past the initial rounds. Don't bother to embarrass yourself"* were some of the things I told myself each time I wanted to try. So, I never did. I said yes to doubt and kept playing small.

As a grown-up now working alongside the Miss Jamaica World Pageant, I sometimes thought back and wondered what could have been if I only had enough self-confidence to move forward.

I recall a conversation with a former contestant and queen a few years ago. While sharing and laughing together, a local media house asked for a picture of us both. We paused, smiled, and took the photograph. When she saw the picture, she said, *"Aisha, look at your smile? Why didn't you enter this competition? You would make a beautiful Queen because you epitomize beauty with a purpose."* She knew nothing about my story and nothing about my past. She also didn't know that those words ricocheted in my heart that night. They brought me back to my twenty-plus-year-old self and rebuilt a part of me that had been broken for years; a part of me that felt unworthy.

My negative self-talk resulted in me avoiding opportunities in the name of self-preservation, but when I identified the root cause (fear) and went back to where I lost self-confidence (when I got fired from that company), I was able to bridge the gap, regain confidence, and fight a little harder every day to not settle. When I finally said yes to possibility, I realized that showing up imperfectly was better than hiding and waiting for perfection.

Avoidance might protect you temporarily, but it steals your momentum and your joy. Every time you say no to an opportunity, you are teaching your brain that fear is in charge.

It's time to break that cycle. Reframe those negative thoughts, shift perspective, and say yes to that scary thing. You'll never know what could happen until you try.

As Shonda Rhimes says in her book, *Year of Yes*, "*[Say] Yes to everything scary. Yes to everything that takes me out of my comfort zone. Yes to everything that feels like it might be crazy. Yes to everything. Everything. Say yes. Yes.*"

It's time for you to silence the inner self-critic, silence negative self-talk, and say yes to possibility.

Ask yourself these questions:

What are some of the negative things that I say to myself that have held me back from a life of excellence and/or the life I really desire?

____

____

____

____

____

____

____

____

What story am I believing that isn't mine? What are my borrowed thoughts and beliefs?

____

____

____

____

____

____

____

____

How can I reframe these negatives and turn them into positives?

What am I saying yes to today?

Comparison Syndrome

Have you ever measured your success against someone else's success? Have you ever measured your messy, behind-the-scenes journey against someone else's flawless Instagram reel or TikTok videos? Ever seen a past colleague's accomplishments and wondered how you aren't as far ahead in life?

Today, we scroll through social media and wonder why our paths feel harder, slower, and less glamorous than those of our counterparts. Why hasn't my breakthrough come yet? Why does everyone else seem to have it all figured out? What's so wrong with me?

I get it! I used to do the very same thing, especially if I thought I was brighter than the other person(s). What we don't see is the struggle hidden in their DMs, the drafts deleted before publication, the sleepless nights they won't ever post about. We almost never see their struggles because we have been so conditioned to curate the perfect lifestyle and publicly broadcast only the best, and I totally understand that it has its place, but it also has its dangers.

I've spoken to and mentored so many teenagers and young women who believed that they were "less than" others simply because they didn't own the designer clothes, jewelry, or other material possessions they saw

their peers, role models, or social media influencers with online.

I've heard conversations about unworthiness among several groups, driven by whether or not you drive, what you drive, where you live, or the size of your home. I've seen people put themselves in unnecessary debt simply to keep up appearances and create and maintain an image that doesn't really align with their reality.

I've lived with the critique and watchful eyes of others because my family did not have the financial wherewithal that others may have had.

Just like many today, I silently compared myself to others. I even questioned why God had to hand me these circumstances in life: *Why couldn't I live there? Why didn't my family have money like others did? Why was I born with the name Ritchie but didn't have the riches to back it up? Why was my life meant to be so hard?* But I have learnt, as Theodore Roosevelt said, that comparison syndrome is really the "thief of joy" and purpose.

Psychologists define social comparisons as our assessment of aspects of our own lives (behaviour, abilities, emotions, business) relative to others. While this can motivate personal growth and self-improvement in many positive ways, it can also be a significant harm to our well-being when treated conversely.

Comparison can steal joy, distort reality, and cause us to measure our worth by someone else's timeline and lifestyle, when in truth, each of our journeys is uniquely different. There is no one born on earth who has experienced life in the exact same way as you have. We may share similar challenges and circumstances, but God created each of us uniquely with unique gifts, abilities, and talents. Our purposes may align or intersect, but they are never identical. This means that we each have our own unique paths to trod, so comparison does not serve us well.

I used to look at the lives of some family members and friends and be truly happy and proud of their progress and success, yet wonder if God had forgotten about me. Some of the people I was supporting with their dreams, goals, and ambitions were winning at life; they were ticking things off their goal lists and vision boards, and I genuinely celebrated them, but silently pondered, *"So, what's up with me? Why wasn't I able to check off those big-ticket items that others were checking off? What was I doing that was so wrong that hindered me from accomplishing some of those things too?"* Comparison was secretly stealing my joy, and that's the

thing: it usually creeps up on you. You look and think unintentionally and silently, until you find yourself unappreciative and stuck in a cycle of complaints because your life doesn't look as nice as the other person's life. There's no joy or winning in that.

One day, I was being introduced to speak at an event. It was a familiar audience, as many people present in the audience already knew me, so I did not provide a speaker bio or introduction because I wasn't really expecting one to be given. Unknown to me, the event organizer had prepared one, which the host delivered. I stood on the sidelines, waiting to walk up to the podium, and as I listened, I felt myself growing very emotional, a wave of gratitude sweeping over my heart. I was busy comparing myself to others based on their material gains and success, without noticing the significant progress I had made personally or the impact I was having on others' lives. I recognized at that moment that my success in that season needed to be different. It was not a measure of how much money I had in my bank account, whether I drove, what I drove, or where I lived—it was something bigger than me, something aligned with the divine purpose God created me for. Having recognized this, I stood on the sidelines and silently thanked God for the progress I had made and for the way He was using me to impact others, whilst seeking forgiveness for my ungratefulness before heading onto the platform.

In my case, I was still working and doing what I was called to do. But if I am totally honest, I may have been able to do even greater things and accomplish more if I had not been so focused on what I did not have because of life's comparisons.

How many of us give up on life and the things we desire because we feel like God forgot about us? How many of us become sluggish in pursuit of our goals because we compare our lives to others? How many of us have stepped out of God's will to chase the things we want because we think it may be taking too long, while others had the things we desired? How many of us have obtained material gains by lowering our standards, morals and/or values because we think we needed that flashy new thing that everybody else seems to have?

It's not worth it!

I've often heard the saying *"Stop comparing your day 1 to someone else's day 100,"* and I wish to endorse that and add: stop comparing your success to someone else's success, because the measure will not always be the same. The only person you are meant to compare yourself to is the version of you that has not dared to begin.

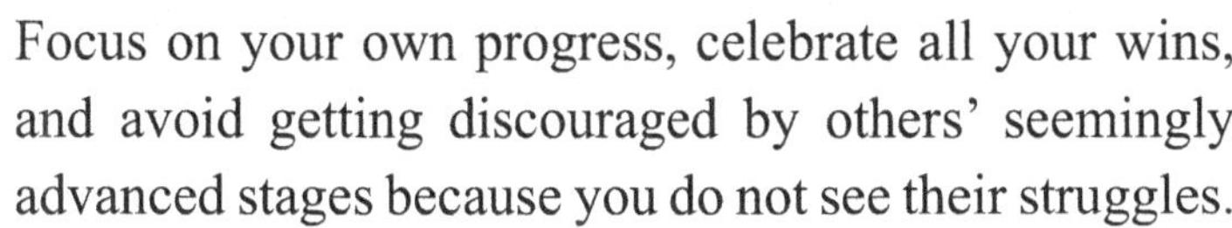

Focus on your own progress, celebrate all your wins, and avoid getting discouraged by others' seemingly advanced stages because you do not see their struggles.

Instead of comparing, be inspired by others and remember that your unique path, with all its ups, downs, and somersaults, is valid and unfolds at its own pace.

Never allow comparison to rob you of gratitude for your own progress. Yes, you may encounter roadblocks and a few detours along the way, but it's not a race. Always remember that the recalibration is ongoing, once you allow God to be your true GPS.

Ask yourself these questions:

How have I allowed comparison to steal my joy?

What do I need to express gratitude for today?

____

____

____

____

____

____

____

____

These self-sabotaging habits don't usually act independently. They generally form and thrive in a toxic environment: procrastination feeds perfectionism, which fuels negative self-talk, leads to avoidance, which is worsened by comparison, and this loops right back into procrastination.

Instead, replace the toxicity with empowering and enabling patterns and beliefs. Seek clarity of mind to avoid procrastination, and let that fuel your courage. This courage invites action, which builds confidence and nurtures self-trust, builds momentum, and thereby replaces procrastination.

These habits try to cage us, but we have the power to break these fear-reinforced bars because God has not

given us a spirit of fear (see 2 Timothy 1:7), and He reinforces this truth throughout His Word, over 100 times, to constantly remind us.

To own your greatness, you must break free from fear and self-sabotage. This is the only way to live in purposeful abundance. It's time to heal and rewire your brain.

Key Takeaways

1. Your journey is not a race.
2. The only person you are meant to compare yourself to is the version of you that has not dared to begin.
3. Avoidance might protect you temporarily, but it steals your momentum, and it steals your joy.

Rich Reasonings

Today I affirm…

Chapter 7

Building Resilience and Antifragility

Congratulations!

You have broken the cage of fear and self-sabotage, so now move forward with renewed direction and clarity. You have acknowledged your rerouted paths, recalibrated, and now navigate seamlessly on a smooth journey to greatness and success. I wish I could tell you that's how life works, but I'm sorry to say it's not. That version is a fairy tale.

The truth is, the path to greatness is not smooth. It is usually a very bumpy road, with potholes, few or no caution signs, and several unexpected and unwelcome detours.

As we journey throughout life, each stage of our growth and development comes with its own unique challenges. Just like the diamond that must go through the fire to bring forth the precious jewel that so many desire, we each have our very own unique fiery darts. Both internal and external forces can affect our ability to own the greatness within. However, the ultimate deciding factor is how we deal with and respond to the challenges when they arise.

What do you tell yourself when life gets hard or when your best plans fail? Are you easy to give up when challenges arise? Do you complain and remain stuck when things don't go your way?

If you hesitated to answer, paused to reflect, or said yes to any of these questions, there's nothing wrong with you—you are just human. All you need to do is flex your resilient muscle a bit more and learn to develop antifragility.

According to the APA Dictionary of Psychology, resilience is *"the process and outcome of successfully adapting to difficult or challenging life experiences, especially through mental, emotional, and behavioral flexibility and adjustment to external and internal demands."* (American Psychological Association, 2018).

While resilience is important, we should aim for more. We should aim to develop antifragility, which is the

true transformation required not only for us to bounce back but also to move forward. Antifragility is a system in which we increase in capability to thrive because of the stressors, shocks, volatility, noise, mistakes, faults, attacks, or failures we experience in life (Taleb, 2012). An antifragile person does not just recover from a setback; they use it as fuel.

Along our rerouted journeys, we sometimes experience adversity, loss, significant stress, and even trauma. Antifragility requires us to access these experiences, adapt to them, and move forward stronger. It does not look like sitting down and giving up. It often looks like sitting and weeping (but not for prolonged periods), then standing on shaking legs. It requires us to re-center ourselves and keep pressing forward.

This is never the easiest thing to do, because, as humans, we dislike pain and generally prefer to control outcomes. We crave the comfort of the known, even if the known is a cage. The easiest thing for us to conclude is that the rerouting was a disaster and that we are not cut out for 'this.' But what if the setback is not a stop sign, but a setup for something greater?

After finally accepting and appreciating the process of motherhood, I began to visualize what it would be like to be a mom. I started to think about the conversations that I would have with my son (yes, I've always wanted a boy, because if it were a girl, how would her hair be combed? There's a reason I have locks). I was excited about having this beautiful little boy, and here he was.

I remember praying my first prayer over this crying baby boy, thanking God for him and praying that God's will for his life be fulfilled. Little did I know that God's will was nothing like I had imagined.

At seventeen months old, he had just started to walk, while several of his peers were walking around even before twelve months old. At two years old, he wasn't speaking very clearly. I started to notice that he was very smart and very clever in some areas, but developmentally slow in others.

I remember us (me and his dad) taking him to a particular preparatory school to enroll him in their Pre-K program. This required that an assessment be carried out to ascertain classroom readiness. This assessment was conducted independently; we were nowhere near him while it was being done.

When the assessor returned, she asked us some interesting questions. She asked us about his development (the same concerns we had), signaling that he was very bright, but his social development was

lacking. Though I had some concerns in the back of my mind, we rejected what her feedback was suggesting; after all, he was a 'COVID-19 baby.' He was born in 2020, just before Jamaica was locked down. He had no siblings and spent two years inside (literally). Of course, he had social development challenges.

So, we tried another school. The school was fine, but the teacher hinted at the same thing, suggesting, as we thought, that it was because of COVID.

Then came another occasion, when he had to visit his pediatrician due to illness. I remember him being timid and scared of almost everything, not responding to his name, and being socially uncomfortable. The doctor recommended that we do a developmental assessment. *Sigh!* This was now the third person who hinted at developmental needs. Doubtful and a little scared to hear the results, we still jumped to it. He was observed over a period of three months: at home, at school, at the assessor's facilities (again independent of us), and was later diagnosed with autism spectrum disorder (Level 1): mild autism. I was now a special needs mom. Really God?!

So many things started to go through my mind. All the things I had visualized for him… for us. *What did this even mean?* I felt so confused. It was as if I didn't de-roll from the last character I played on stage, the mother of a special needs son, which resulted from an unplanned and unexpected pregnancy.

A flood of questions and thoughts bombarded my mind. I wondered what I had done wrong during the pregnancy or before for this to happen to me and to him. I wondered if I jinxed myself when I had a conversation during the pregnancy with his dad about what would have happened if the child were disabled or special needs. I wondered why God would really do this to me. *Was it punishment because I had sex before marriage? Why was He putting me in another stressful and unpleasant situation? Why did it feel like He had left me? Why was He silent about all the questions I was asking?*

In that raw, heartbreaking moment, a profound choice presented itself; one in which I could choose to forge resilience into antifragility. I could resist this rerouting, fight the diagnosis, and live in the "why" and denial, or I could lean into it, not with understanding, but with trust, embracing my new parental path.

As I hugged my beaming two-year-old son with tears running down my cheeks, I recalled the prayer I prayed when He was born, asking God to have His way in his life; the prayer where I accepted that His will would be done. A familiar peace came over me; it was the peace

I felt when I accepted that He would make something beautiful out of my mess.

I smiled with tears in my eyes, and I looked at my son and said, *"You're going to be just fine."* I sang the song He had placed on my heart and lips during the pregnancy, *"Something beautiful, something good..."* I didn't understand why, but I somehow understood that it was God's will, and that all I had to do was provide for him in the best way possible.

We immediately sought early intervention, and God's favour was upon us because within just a few weeks, he enrolled in the necessary therapy sessions. This is extremely uncommon in Jamaica, as it usually takes months, and in some cases years, to get enrolled in these programs due to the scarcity of resources and expertise in this area. But God already had it planned for him. He had already mapped the path. He had already positioned some key enablers in my son's life that would ensure that he was not delayed or denied. He was already on the case and had already gone before us on this journey.

You see, God sees, knows, and understands our needs. He can see everything miles and miles in advance of what we can. The problem is that in our short-sightedness, we try to see end-to-end, but that's literally impossible. All He asks is that we trust Him.

Proverbs 3:5–6 tells us to *"Trust in the Lord with all thine heart; and lean not unto thine own understanding. In all thy ways acknowledge him, and he shall direct thy paths." (KJV).*

When we trust in God, He promises to direct our path. Notice, He didn't say that He would make it easy; He said He would make it purposeful. It may seem crooked, bumpy, windy, messy, and sometimes uncomfortable, but He still asks us to trust Him. Our understanding sees the bumpy detour, but His guidance sees the necessary terrain for our transformation.

Today, I have a brilliant five-year-old son whom I absolutely adore and am so very proud of; a son who reminds me every day about Jesus and His faithfulness (Yes, he actually says this to me every single day); a son who walks in and infects every room he enters with pure love and joy to people known and unknown.

I recognized that what the world labels a disability is actually his superpower, not just because of his vast knowledge base, many talents, and unique interests, but because of the pure, unfiltered light he carries: the light of God.

The stressor of the diagnosis did not just create a resilient mother who copes; it forged an antifragile

woman who sees the world, my son, and my own purpose with deeper clarity, advocacy, and love.

I'm sure this story is still being written as our journey continues, but I am confident that once He guides and directs, we will be fine. So as bumpy as it might be, I continue to trust in the unfailing hand of God.

Life can throw many things at us, but to develop the antifragility necessary to move forward amidst hardships and adversity, God must be our guide. It is impossible for us to do it by ourselves. We need Him to strengthen us day by day, seal the pits and trenches, and open new avenues for us to thrive and achieve success, so stop asking *"Why me?"* and instead ask *"What are You trying to build in me?"* This is where antifragility is cultivated.

Your rerouting is not a denial of your destiny; it is the delivery route for a version of yourself capable of fulfilling it. Remember, the fire not only tests the diamond, but it also creates the conditions that allow it to exist, so trust the process. The path may be bumpy, but it is uniquely yours. You are being built up, stronger, wiser, and more formidable than ever before, and that is the ultimate set-up for a greatness that no smooth road could ever have led you to.

Key Takeaways

1. Your rerouting is not a denial of your destiny; it is the delivery route for a version of yourself capable of fulfilling it.
2. [Your] setback is not a stop sign, but a setup for something greater.

Rich Reasonings

Reframe your setback as setup. Assess how this new territory or experience has or can open opportunities for you to grow and succeed that the smooth road would never have exposed you to. In your reflection, identify any actions that you need to take today to develop antifragility.

Chapter 8

Step Into Your Greatness

Unfortunately, sometimes the detours we experience in life do not end when they should because we claim we are waiting on God, when the truth is, it lingers because God is waiting on us.

We can spend years trapped in cyclical rerouted paths, replaying pain, revisiting disappointment, questioning time and even God, wondering if and when success will ever find us, while holding the very "keys" meant to unlock our next season. This is something that the enemy uses to keep us stuck.

You do not need more preparation. You do not need another sign. You do not need to wait until the fear disappears. You have already been adequately prepared and built for your next, more thriving season. The setbacks shaped you. The delays refined you. The detours trained you. Absolutely nothing that you went through was arbitrary; nothing is wasted.

The Bible tells us that *faith without works is dead* (see James 2:17). This means that hope, wishing, and even belief alone will not take us there. Trust must be partnered with action. Author Roseanna White supports this as she writes in her article *Faith is a Verb,* "*It's important to realize that faith is not just something we hold in our hearts or our minds or our souls, wherever it rightly lives. Faith is something we act on. Faith is something we DO.*" (White, 2024). Behavioral psychology further supports this by stating that momentum often follows action rather than motivation. We move first, then confidence catches up.

All of this points to one conclusion: **greatness is not something that falls into our laps. It is something we step into.**

Here is a framework I use to help me when doubt creeps in and I feel tempted to shrink back or even fall back into the cyclical trap of reliving past pain. It reminds me that owning greatness, the one I was created with and predestined for, requires self-belief and deliberate and courageous action.

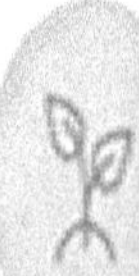

The REROUTE Framework

R - Reclaim Your Story
E - Engage Your Faith
R - Release Fear and Perfection
O Own Your Authority
U – Use What's in Your Hands
T – Take the Risk
E - Expect Growth, Not Ease

Reclaim Your Story

Appreciate your journey. Stop thinking about it as a liability. It is exactly the opposite: an asset.

Your experiences have given you wisdom, built resilience and antifragility, and perspective that could only be experiential. The roadblocks and detours that you survived did not disqualify you, they equipped you. Your growth shows that you have gained increased strength, deepened purpose, and clarified priorities because of your adversities.

Reframe and reclaim the narrative. You are not behind. You are not broken. You are not defeated. You are exactly where God wants you to be: you are becoming exactly who He called you to be.

Action Step: Go back to the journey map you did before. Now, take some time to identify how each detour has strengthened you.

Detour	Lesson Learnt and Strengths Gained

Engage Your Faith

Trusting God requires us to activate our faith. This means we must take intentional faith steps to realize all that He has planned for us. Stop spiritualizing stagnation; God is prompting you to move.

Remember, God cannot bless what you do not do. Instead, your blessing is tied to obedience and action. You do your part, and God will handle the rest. Faith moves when you move.

Action Step: What step(s) have you been avoiding because they seem too risky? Answer honestly, then take action.

Release Fear and Perfection

Fear will always have an opinion on how you choose to live and show up in this world, but remember, they are lies.

Perfection will also demand more time to get everything right and ready for flawless execution, even tricking you into avoidance, but remember, you are equipped.

If you wait until you feel ready, you will probably never move. Remember that the antidote for fear is initiative, so rewire your brain today. Train it to feel safer and more comfortable in spite of being fearful through the consistent actions you take daily.

We often hear the phrase *"faith over fear,"* but remember, too, that faith is an action word. Start moving. Started getting things done. Silence fear and embrace success. Progress is always better than perfection.

Action Steps: What is one imperfect step that you can commit to taking today?

____

____

____

____

____

____

____

____

____

____

____

Name your fears and combat them with an affirming truth.

____

____

____

____

____

____

____

Fear	**Truth and/or Affirmation**

Own Your Authority

You don't need permission to live in purpose and abundance. God has already given you everything you need. From the moment you were conceived, you were created with unique abilities to be used for the accomplishment of your divine purpose. This means that you were predestined for greatness. There is nothing ordinary about you. God created and fashioned you exactly the way He wanted to, and He says it is good. You don't need to seek the validation or permission of others to shine. God entrusted you, and only you, with His blessings and direction. He gave you imagination, visualization, and the ability to manifest what He has called you to do. So, forget what others may think or say.

Step up and own the authority! Quiet the doubting inner critic. Stop minimizing your talents and the skills you have developed along your journey. Forget the noise around you. Forget the world's approval. Your journey and vision were uniquely given to you. It does not need to be audited or validated by anyone because God has already validated you.

Power and purpose lives inside you. Walk proudly and boldly in your God-given identity.

Action Step: In which area of your life will you decide to step up and own your authority? How could this manifest as your greatest success?

Use What You Have In Your Hands

Stop complaining about needing more resources. *What do you have in your hand?* Moses had a shepherd's staff, David had a sling, and Joseph could interpret dreams. *What has God given you that can be used to accomplish your greatest success?*

Remember, you have gifts, talents, skills, experiences, connections, and ideas right now that can be utilized to fuel your breakthrough. What you have is already good enough to get started. Use it!

Action Step: Create a resource bank. How can you utilise these to accomplish the success you desire?

Skill, Talent, Experience, etc.	**How can this be leveraged?**

Take the Risk

Bet on yourself. Take a leap of faith. Growth not only requires discomfort, but it also requires risk. In fact, every meaningful shift requires some kind of risk; not recklessness, but faith steps that say I'm scared, but I am moving anyway. This is where greatness separates itself from mediocrity.

You survived your rerouted paths and all the anxiety and difficulties that came with it for a reason. You survived so that you can live purposefully. Stop postponing your success. Take the risk.

Action Step: Review the risk actions you named above and name one risky action that you will be taking. State how this action may change your entire life.

____

____

____

____

____

____

____

____

____

Expect Growth, Not Ease

Owning and stepping into greatness does not mean the journey suddenly becomes smooth. Remember, each stage of growth requires trial and refinement.

Stepping into greatness simply means you are becoming stronger, more resilient, and antifragile. True antifragility is not built by resisting challenges or avoiding difficulties; it is built by walking through them with conviction, clarity, and faith.

Pressure may hurt you, but it will not break you; instead, it will build you. Expect growth and stretching, but more than anything else, expect and believe in your victory.

Action Step: Where are you currently experiencing growth in your life? Express gratitude for all it has taught you.

____

____

____

____

____

____

____

____

____

____

Everything you have experienced in life has brought you to this point. Your unique journey has led you to exactly where you need to be. It's time for you to act now in order to step into your greatness.

Step forward boldly and audaciously—knowing and trusting that God has your back and has your best interest at heart. Your rerouted path was not a rejection; it was redirection to something greater.

Conclusion

If you have made it this far, you are not here by accident. Every chapter you have read, every story you have connected with, every moment that made you pause and reflect has been leading to this moment. This is not just the end of the book, but the beginning of a decision to step into your greatness.

You may have begun this book with questions and disappointments. Your life may have felt misaligned, as if everything you envisioned, planned, or pursued has gone completely sideways. Plans changed, timing unraveled, and the well-thought-out journey you planned ended up in shambles, with nothing making sense. Yet, here you are. You are still standing, still pressing, and still believing, even if it's in fragments.

This book was never meant to convince you that detours are easy; it is meant to demonstrate that they are divine. I acknowledge that these unplanned and unprepared reroutes sometimes cost us confidence, momentum, and even relationships; my own personal reroutes have demonstrated that vividly. However, I must also acknowledge that what may seem like setbacks are not signs of failure but are usually evidence that life carries intention beyond our own understanding.

Perhaps what has felt like road closures or detours has begun to reveal itself as a setup for greater alignment with your purpose, and slowly, something formidable is forming within you.

You were never lost in these rerouted paths; you were always being led because God's light and presence have always been there with you. Understanding the journey is not enough. You must move. You must move from awareness to purpose activation. This requires you to take the necessary faith steps.

You don't step into greatness accidentally; you step into it intentionally. You have to make the choice. Navigating the road ahead will require courage, acknowledging that there will still be moments when fear tries to convince you to shrink back, but remember you are now wiser, stronger, and antifragile. You have already proven that you can endure and overcome uncomfortable and difficult paths.

God has done the forming. Life has done the refining. Now you step with greatness as your hallmark.

This is the moment where you stop seeing your past as something to recover from, and start recognising it as something that prepared you for your next, more thriving season. You don't need the full map; you just need to trust the One who created the map and take the next step.

Your life has been purposely rerouted so step forward with clarity and confidence, knowing that greatness is your birthright and that greatness is ahead of you.

About the Author

Aisha Ritchie is a purpose-driven impact creator, international speaker, author, certified Christian life and business coach, and creative. Born and raised in the inner city of Kingston, Jamaica, Aisha defied the odds to build a life and career rooted in impact, proving that where you begin does not determine where you can go. With a deep passion for personal growth and purposeful living, she empowers individuals to break free from limiting beliefs, embrace their God-given identity, and unlock the abundance that comes with living intentionally. Her work blends lived experience, practical insight, and faith-rooted wisdom in a way that is both relatable and transformative. Her message resonates across diverse platforms, from private coaching sessions, corporate workshops, and conferences to global webinars, where she blends expertise with heart to inspire lasting change.

References

American Psychological Association. (2018, April 19). *American Psychological Association*. Retrieved from American Psychological Association: https://dictionary.apa.org/resilience

Beckman, M. (2003, October 9). *Rejection Is Like Pain to the Brain.* Retrieved from Science: https://www.science.org/content/article/rejection-pain-brain#:~:text=Social%20exclusion%20activates%20the%20same%20regions%20as%20physical%20pain&text=Those%20hurt%20feelings%20when%20you,it%20responds%20to%20physical%20pain.

Cambridge Advanced Learner's Dictionary & Thesaurus. (2025). *Cambridge Dictionary.* Retrieved from Cambridge Dictionary: https://dictionary.cambridge.org/dictionary/english/panic

Jones, N. (2024). *The Gift of Rejection: Harness Your Pain to Propel Your Purpose.* Zondervan.

Kendra Cherry, M. (2025, September 29). *What Is Procrastination? Why we keep putting things off, despite the consequences.* Retrieved from VeryWell Mind: https://www.verywellmind.com/the-psychology-of-procrastination-2795944

Rhimes, S. (2015). *Year of Yes: How to Dance It Out, Stand in the Sun and Be Your Own Person.* New York, USA: Simon & Schuster.

Scott, E. (2023, November 22). *The Toxic Effects of Negative Self-Talk.* Retrieved from Verywell Mind: https://www.verywellmind.com/negative-self-talk-and-how-it-affects-us-4161304

Stephanie Booth and Smitha Bhandari, M. (2025, February 11). Imposter Syndrome: How to Overcome It. United States.

Taleb, N. N. (2012). *Antifragile.* United Kingdom: Penguin.

White, R. (2024, June 20). *Faith is a Verb.* Retrieved from www.roseannamwhite.com: https://www.roseannamwhite.com/2024/06/faith-is-a-verb.html

www.ingramcontent.com/pod-product-compliance
Lightning Source LLC
LaVergne TN
LVHW010835120826
845149LV00016B/2559
9781966723493